A LOOK AT THE BILL OF RIGHTS

Freedom to ASSEMBLE

BY MARY GRIFFIN

CRASHCOURSE

Gareth Stevens PUBLISHING

Please visit our website, www.garethstevens.com. For a free color catalog of all our high-quality books, call toll free 1-800-542-2595 or fax 1-877-542-2596.

Library of Congress Cataloging-in-Publication Data
Names: Griffin, Mary, 1978- author.
Title: Freedom to assemble / Mary Griffin.
Description: Buffalo, New York : Gareth Stevens Publishing, 2026. | Series: A look at the bill of rights | Includes index.
Identifiers: LCCN 2024031190 | ISBN 9781482470352 (library binding) | ISBN 9781482470345 (paperback) | ISBN 9781482470369 (ebook)
Subjects: LCSH: Assembly, Right of–United States–Juvenile literature. | United States. Constitution. 1st Amendment–Juvenile literature. | Freedom of expression–United States–Juvenile literature. | Civil rights–United States–Juvenile literature. | Protest movements–United States–Juvenile literature.
Classification: LCC KF4778 .G75 2026 | DDC 342.7308/54–dc23/eng/20240714
LC record available at https://lccn.loc.gov/2024031190

First Edition

Published in 2026 by
Gareth Stevens Publishing
2544 Clinton Street
Buffalo, NY 14224

Designer: Andrea Davison-Bartolotta
Editor: Kristen Rajczak Nelson

Photo credits: Cover, p. 1 Jelani Photography/Shutterstock.com; series art (interior background texture) Nik Merkulov/Shutterstock.com; series art (fact box sticker) Sulovsky/Shutterstock.com; series art (blue backgrounds) Le Chernina/Shutterstock.com; series art (banners) saicle/Shutterstock.com; p. 5 (inset) Everett Collection/Shutterstock.com; pp. 5 (main), 17 courtesy of Library of Congress; p. 7 (bottom) File:Scene at the Signing of the Constitution of the United States.jpg/Wikimedia Commons; p. 7 (top) courtesy of the National Archives; p. 9 (Masison) File:James Madison 1816.jpg/Wikimedia Commons; p. 9 (frame) Theeradech Sanin/Shutterstock.com; p. 9 (bottom) ungvar/Shutterstock.com; p. 11 Zsuzsi Matolcsy/Shutterstock.com; p. 13 Foolish Productions/Shutterstock.com; p. 15 loreanto/Shutterstock.com; p. 19 (top) Fred Schilling, Collection of the Supreme Court of the United States/ File:Supreme Court of the United States - Roberts Court 2022.jpg/Wikimedia Commons; p. 19 (bottom) Doppioclick/Shutterstock.com; p. 21 (all) Sebastian Portillo/Shutterstock.com; p. 23 John YE/Shutterstock.com; p. 25 (bottom) Andrey_Popov/Shutterstock.com; p. 25 (top) Rawpixel.com/Shutterstock.com; p. 27 Ground Picture/Shutterstock.com; p. 29 Volodymyr TVERDOKHLIB/Shutterstock.com.

Printed in China

CPSIA compliance information: Batch #QS26GS: For further information contact Gareth Stevens at 1-800-542-2595.

Contents

Words in the glossary appear in **bold** type the first time they are used in the text.

AN IMPORTANT RIGHT

During the **American Revolution**, groups of colonists assembled, or gathered, to make plans. They met in public to voice their problems with the British government. Early in the founding of the United States, it was clear that being able to assemble should be a **citizen**'s right.

Make the GRADE

Colonists live in a colony, or land controlled by another country. One colonial revolutionary group was the Sons of Liberty, founded by Samuel Adams.

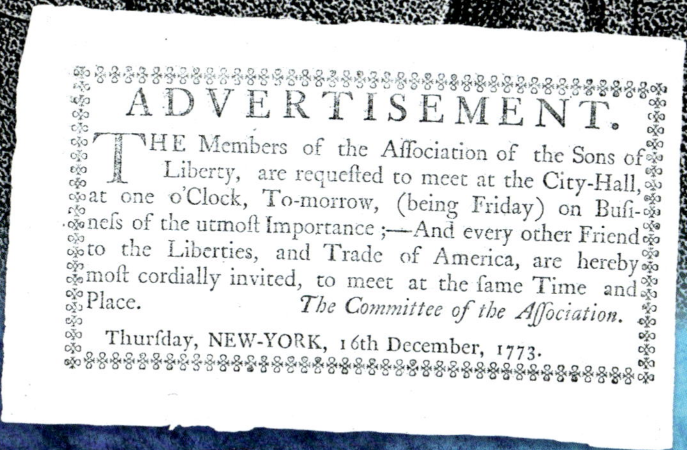

ADVERTISEMENT.

THE Members of the Aſſociation of the Sons of Liberty, are requeſted to meet at the City-Hall, at one o'Clock, To-morrow, (being Friday) on Buſineſs of the utmoſt Importance;—And every other Friend to the Liberties, and Trade of America, are hereby moſt cordially invited, to meet at the ſame Time and Place.

The Committee of the Aſſociation.

Thurſday, NEW-YORK, 16th December, 1773.

The U.S. Constitution didn't have a list of citizens' rights at first. Some leaders wouldn't sign the Constitution without one. A few states didn't want to approve, or agree to, the Constitution without the promise that it would be added.

Make the GRADE

A constitution is a list of the basic laws of a country or state. The U.S. Constitution has been in use since 1789.

...ventions of nine States, shall be sufficient for the Establishment of this Constitution between the States

done in Convention by the Unanimous Consent of the States present the Seventeenth Day of September in the Year of our Lord one thousand seven hundred and Eighty seven and of the Independance of the United States of America the Twelfth In witness whereof We have hereunto subscribed our Names,

Go. Washington—Presidt. and deputy from Virginia

Delaware: Geo: Read, Gunning Bedford jun, John Dickinson, Richard Bassett, Jaco: Broom

Maryland: James McHenry, Dan of St Thos. Jenifer, Danl Carroll

Virginia: John Blair—, James Madison Jr.

North Carolina: Wm. Blount, Richd. Dobbs Spaight, Hu Williamson

South Carolina: J. Rutledge, Charles Cotesworth Pinckney, Charles Pinckney, Pierce Butler

Georgia: William Few, Abr Baldwin

New Hampshire: John Langdon, Nicholas Gilman

Massachusetts: Nathaniel Gorham, Rufus King

Connecticut: Wm. Saml. Johnson, Roger Sherman

New York: Alexander Hamilton

New Jersey: Wil: Livingston, David Brearley, Wm. Paterson, Jona: Dayton

Pensylvania: B Franklin, Thomas Mifflin, Robt. Morris, Geo. Clymer, Thos. FitzSimons, Jared Ingersoll, James Wilson, Gouv Morris

signatures on the U.S. Constitution

THE FIRST AMENDMENTS

In June 1789, James Madison presented amendments, or changes, to the Constitution to the first U.S. Congress. The amendments listed rights that would be guaranteed, or promised, to citizens. The states approved 10 of the amendments. Today, they are called the Bill of Rights.

Make the GRADE

James Madison became the fourth U.S. president. He served from 1809 to 1817.

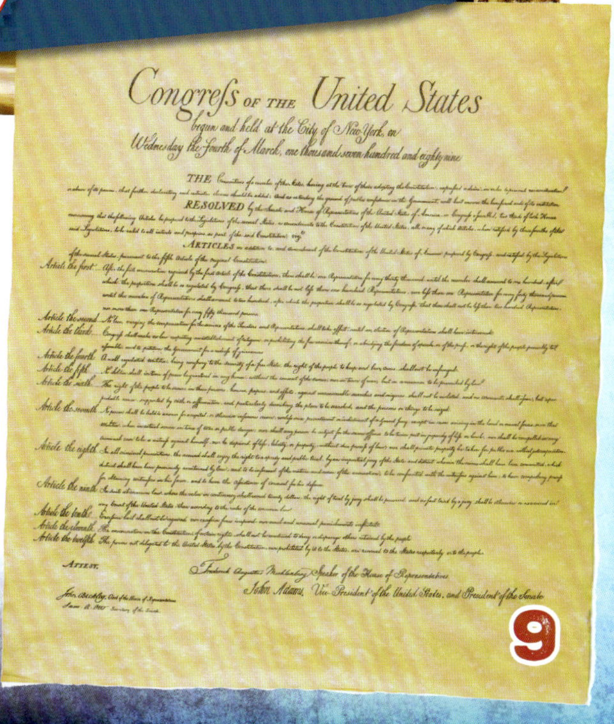
Congress of the United States
begun and held at the City of New-York, on
Wednesday the fourth of March, one thousand seven hundred and eighty nine

Bill of Rights

WHAT DOES IT SAY?

The First Amendment says in part: "Congress shall make no law . . . abridging . . . the right of the people peaceably to assemble." This means the government cannot stop citizens from gathering peacefully. It also means no laws can be made that **weaken** this right.

Make the GRADE

The First Amendment also guarantees citizens' rights to practice any religion, or faith, they want, and freedom of speech, among other rights.

PROTEST!

The freedom to assemble also means the freedom to protest. Protesting is when citizens speak out about problems or laws they don't like. Events, or happenings, where these ideas are shared are called protests too. Groups may gather to share any beliefs they want to.

Make the GRADE

Counterprotests are protected under the First Amendment too. This is when citizens protest another protest!

Even citizens with **unpopular** views have the right to assemble and protest. The government cannot stop them even if it does not agree with their message. This allows for all sides of an **issue** to be heard.

Make the GRADE

The rights to freedom of speech, press, and assembly are closely tied. In general, these rights stop the government from jailing or fining citizens for what they say or write, or for taking part in gatherings.

FEAR LESS
LOVE MORE

ASSEMBLY IN HISTORY

The freedom to assemble has long been a way Americans make their voices heard. In the early 1900s, women worked to get the right to vote using their right to assemble. During the **civil rights movement** of the 1950s and 1960s, protests made **segregation** national news.

Make the GRADE

More than 200,000 people assembled as part of the March on Washington for Jobs and Freedom on August 28, 1963. This was an important day during the civil rights movement.

THE COURT'S ROLE

The Supreme Court is the highest court in the United States. It hears cases that have to do with citizens' rights, such as the freedom of assembly. It decides whether laws and government actions are constitutional, which means they follow the U.S. Constitution.

Supreme Court justices, 2022

Make the GRADE

A big part of the Supreme Court's job is interpreting the meaning of the Constitution. Interpret means to tell the meaning of something.

Supreme Court building

KEEPING THE PEACE

One part of the Constitution is clear as written: only peaceful gatherings are **protected** by the First Amendment. Over time, Supreme Court decisions have interpreted this right further. It has said the planning of a peaceful gathering or protest is also protected by the First Amendment.

Make the GRADE

Violent protests or **riots**, such as those on January 6, 2021, in Washington, DC, are not protected by the First Amendment.

ON PUBLIC PROPERTY

Gatherings on public property, which means owned by the government, are protected by the First Amendment right to assemble. This includes public **colleges**. In 2024, college students across the United States protested colleges' ties to Israel while it was at war.

student protest at the University of Minnesota, April 2024

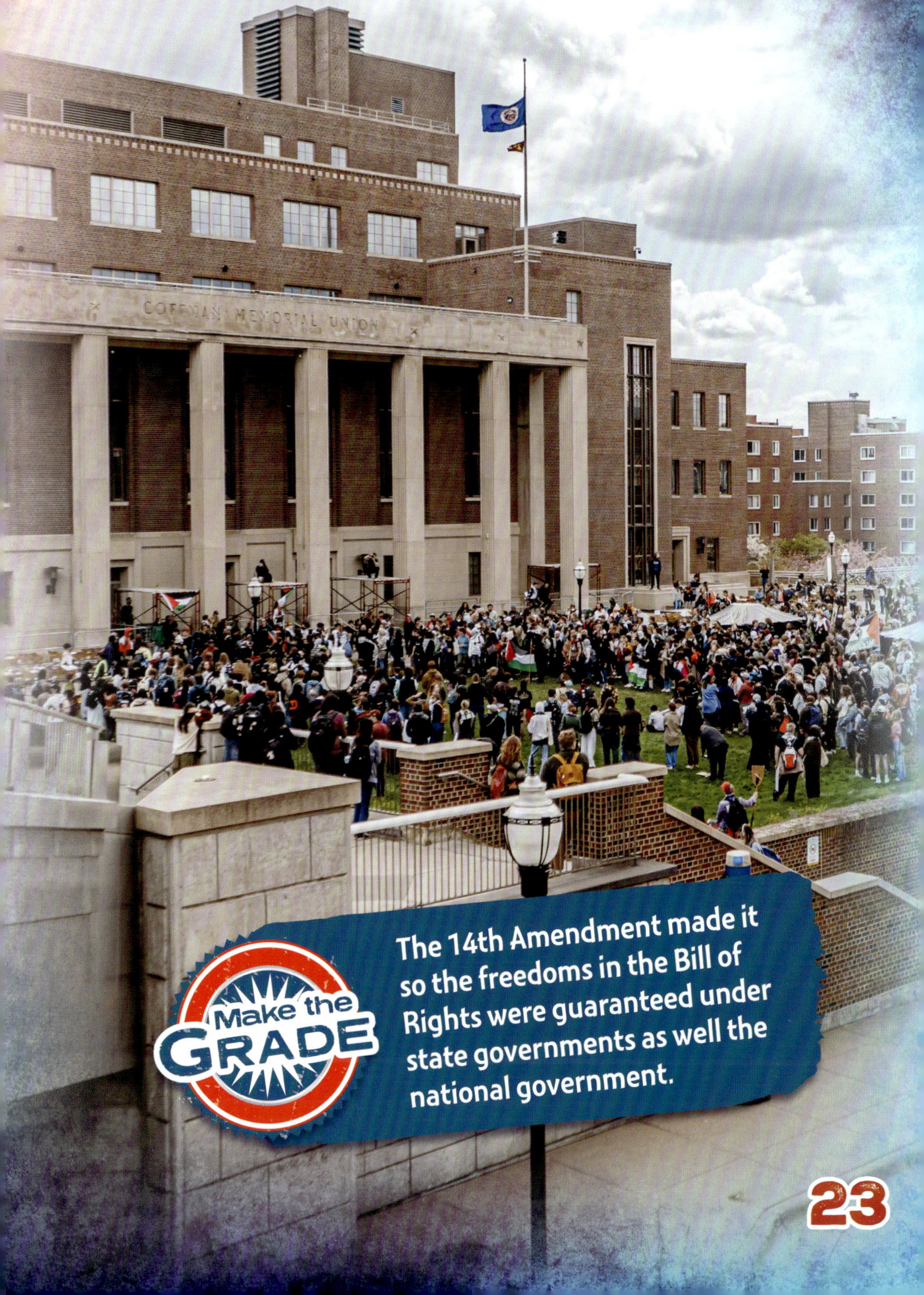

Make the GRADE

The 14th Amendment made it so the freedoms in the Bill of Rights were guaranteed under state governments as well the national government.

PERMITS PERMITTED

One common way the government **limits** freedom of assembly is to require a permit for certain gatherings, such as parades and protests. This is constitutional if the permit requirements are the same for every group. The requirements can't be too hard to meet either.

Make the GRADE

A permit is a document, or official paper, saying a person or group is allowed to do something.

REASONABLE LIMITS

The government may make other rules about gatherings if they are fair and apply to everyone. At times, it can limit the time, place, or manner of a gathering. These limits have to have a good reason, such as keeping a large gathering from blocking a building's entrance.

Make the GRADE

Unless there is a real chance of a riot and violence, or a group is blocking cars on the road, even the police cannot break up a peaceful gathering.

GET TOGETHER!

The freedom to assemble is special. It is a right that is for more than just one person! That means it's a powerful way for citizens to have their voices heard. It allows groups to loudly ask for change by working together.

Make the GRADE

Families may go to protests or other peaceful gatherings together. See if there is a gathering in your town you'd like to take part in.

FAMOUSLY ASSEMBLED

The freedom of assembly has long been used in the United States to ask for change or protest the government. Here are some famous examples.

Women's Suffrage Parade, March 3, 1913

Thousands of women marched in Washington, DC, in favor of giving women suffrage, or the right to vote.

The Children's Crusade, May 2, 1963

More than 1,000 students took to the streets of Birmingham, Alabama, to protest for civil rights for Black Americans. Hundreds were jailed for their actions.

White House Peace Vigil

This ongoing protest started in 1981. It takes place in the park across the street from the White House. It is about issues like human rights or weapons, sometimes called arms.

Commitment March, August 28, 2020

Thousands marched in Washington, DC, in protest of police treatment of Black Americans.

Glossary

American Revolution: The war in which the colonies won their freedom from England.

citizen: Someone who lives in a country legally and has certain rights.

civil rights movement: A time period in U.S. history starting in the 1950s in which African Americans fought for equal civil rights, or the freedoms granted to us by law.

college: A school after high school.

issue: An important topic that people care about.

limit: To stop something from being larger, longer, or more.

protect: To keep safe.

riot: A public disturbance during which a group of angry people become noisy and out of control.

segregation: The forced separation of races or classes.

unpopular: Not liked by many people.

violent: Having to do with the use of force to harm someone.

weaken: To make less strong.

For More Information

Books

Matulli, Allison, and Clelia Castro-Malaspina. *Your Freedom, Your Power: A Kid's Guide to the First Amendment.* Philadelphia, PA: Running Press Kids, 2023.

Keppeler, Jill. *What Is the First Amendment?* Buffalo, NY: Rosen Publishing, 2023.

Website

The Bill of Rights
https://www.archives.gov/founding-docs/bill-of-rights/what-does-it-say
Find out more about each of the first 10 amendments to the U.S. Constitution here.

Index